GUIDE WITH RECONSTRUCTIONS
ANCIENT ROME

past and present

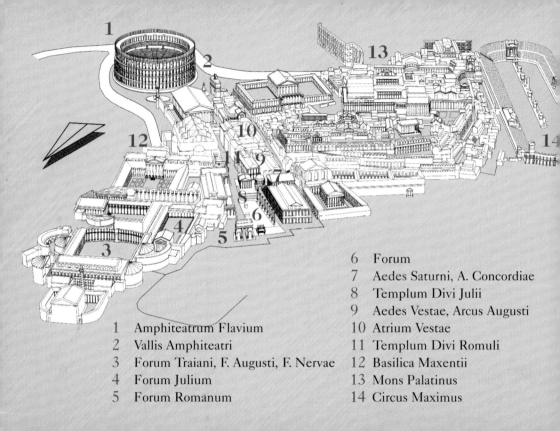

1 Amphiteatrum Flavium
2 Vallis Amphiteatri
3 Forum Traiani, F. Augusti, F. Nervae
4 Forum Julium
5 Forum Romanum
6 Forum
7 Aedes Saturni, A. Concordiae
8 Templum Divi Julii
9 Aedes Vestae, Arcus Augusti
10 Atrium Vestae
11 Templum Divi Romuli
12 Basilica Maxentii
13 Mons Palatinus
14 Circus Maximus

THE MONUMENTS OF ROME

from the Village of Huts on the Palatine to the Cosmopolitan City on the Banks of the Tiber.

The floors of the two or three huts cut out of the rock of the Palatine and the simple earth graves of a burial ground, the Sepulcretum, on the edge of the Forum are the earliest traces that we can find today of what was later to become Rome, her most ancient 'monuments' as it were.

One of the several small villages which had sprang up on these hills separated by broad marshes, the one on the Palatine controlled the Tiber crossing and the market which had long existed on the left bank of the river. This constituted the nucleus around which the other inhabited areas began to concentrate between the 8th and the 7th centuries BC, giving rise over time to the actual city.

By the 6th century it was already encircled by walls and protected by a fortified strong point on the Capitoline, it boasted a landing stage on the Tiber and a commercial and political center in the Forum, and it was enriched by public buildings and sanctuaries (most notably the Temple of Jupiter Optimus Maximus Capitolinus).

Over the course of next century the city grew to include the Aventine, and in the first half of the 4th century, following recovery from the invasion of the Gauls and the ruin it had left in its wake, a new circle of walls was erected to protect an extensive urban area, which now covered over 400 hectares.

After the conquest of the Greek East (2nd -1st century BC), entire districts were built or redesigned along the lines of eastern cities: Greek architectural models were adopted, such as the public porticus, and new ones were invented, such as the basilica, to house the law courts. The systematic application of arch and vault made it possible to erect ever larger and more functional buildings, such as the commercial porticoes of the vast district known as the Emporium, south of the Aventine. Between 179 and 142 BC, the first stone bridge was built over the Tiber (Pons Aemilius). The 2nd century also saw a start being made with the building up of the Campus Martius, when the first porticoes and temples were erected; Pompey's projects in the next century (porticoes and a theater) made it the city's natural and most important area of expansion.

In the 1st century BC, town planning and public building became an explicit part of the political agenda of the heads of state, from Sulla to Pompey and Caesar. The only one of Caesar's grand building projects to survive his death was the construction of a new Forum, the first step in the creation of the monumental complex that the Imperial Fora were later to become. Caesar's successor, Augustus, brought to completion many of the buildings left unfinished (such as the Basilica Julia, the Theater of Marcellus and the Curia). He also built another forum and liberally decorated the Campus Martius with public and private buildings, aided by his helpers, first and foremost among whom was Agrippa: these range from the Theater of Balbus to the Amphitheater of Statilius Taurus, from the Baths of Agrippa to the first Pantheon, and from the Altar of Peace (Ara Pacis) to the Augustan Sundial, and culminate in the grandiose mausoleum erected for the imperial family. And it was also Augustus who, by choosing to live on the Palatine, determined the transformation of the hill into the single magnificent imperial residence of later days.

After the terrible fire of 64 AD, which razed to the ground a large part of the city, Nero trans-

General view of Via dei Fori Imperiali and of the valley of the Colosseum

formed a good part of the center into a splendid villa, the Domus Aurea (Golden House), and initiated a systematic project for the rebuilding of the city, which can only be said to have been completed under the Flavian dynasty, with Domitian's intense building work and after Vespasian and Titus had, between 75 and 80, erected the building which would become the symbol of Rome: the Flavian Amphitheater or Colosseum.

The 2nd century AD marked the culmination of Rome's city-planning and building activity. It is to this period that we may trace Trajan's Baths and Forum, the magnificent temples such as that of Venus and Roma, the new Pantheon, the Mausoleum of Hadrian across the Tiber and the two spectacular spiral columns engraved with the exploits of their patrons. Meanwhile in the private sector, multistorey tenements (insulae) were extensively built, often to form genuine neighborhoods.

In the 3rd century there was a general slowing down of activity, notwithstanding the building of the Baths of Caracalla. In 275 AD Aurelian responded to the growing barbarian menace on the frontiers of the empire by ordering the building of a new circle of city walls, 18km in circumference, which nonetheless contained the greatest, wealthiest and most monumental city yet to be seen on the face of the earth.

But building in the city did not come to a complete halt; the Baths of Diocletian and the Basilica of Maxentius, opened by Constantine in 312 AD, constituted two more fantastic chapters in the history of Roman architecture, now spanning back over a thousand years. A little later, the Arch of Constantine, erected in his honour by the Senate in 315 with the recycling of material from older monuments was to mark the end of an era. Indeed, Constantinople, which was to be the empire's new capital, the 'New Rome', was founded on the shores of the Bosphorus on 11 May 330 AD.

The Arch of Titus, built to celebrate the triumph of the Emperor for the conquest of Jerusalem

THE COLOSSEUM

The Colosseum, which in its day was known as the Flavian Amphitheater, was built in the middle of the broad valley between the Palatine, Caelian and Esquiline hills, where Nero had sited the lake in the gardens of his Domus Aurea. As for its imposing size, the figures speak for themselves: the major axis of its elliptical plan is 188m long, the minor axis attains 156m, and the walls in the outer ring rise to almost 50m above ground; more than 100,000 cubic meters of travertine were used to build it and even the metal pins that held the blocks together must have weighed more than 300 tons.

Begun by Vespasian shortly after 70 AD, the amphitheater was opened by Titus ten years later. The ceremonies and games on that occasion went on for a hundred days and some 5000 wild animals were put to death during that time. The eighty arches at ground level were progressively numbered (the number corresponding to that on the spectator's tessera or admission card) and led, via a system of internal corridors, to the 160 outlets (*vomitoria*) that took the visitor to his place on the steps of the *cavea*, which was borne up by arches and vaults.

Beside the amphitheater stood the **Colossus of Nero**,

a giant statue of gilt bronze, 30 m high, work of the Greek sculptor Zenodoros. It originally represented the emperor, but after his death was modified to depict the sun god. The interior of the Colosseum consisted of the arena, a wooden floor bearing a bed of sand and covering an area of about 76 m by 46 m, and the stands or *cavea*, subdivided into three superimposed sectors of steps crowned on high by a 'loggia' that housed a fourth order of steps, made of wood and providing the standing room. Each sector of the *cavea* was rigorously reserved for a particular class of citizens, the places on top being assigned to the least important, though all enjoyed free entry. Counting also the standing spectators, the amphitheater could accommodate about 70,000 people, who came there to watch gladiatorial combats and wild beast hunts as well as less important spectacles of various kinds. An enormous awning protected the spectators from the heat of the sun; it's segments were hoisted by a special detachment

Mosaic with a hunting scene (Sousse-Tunisia)

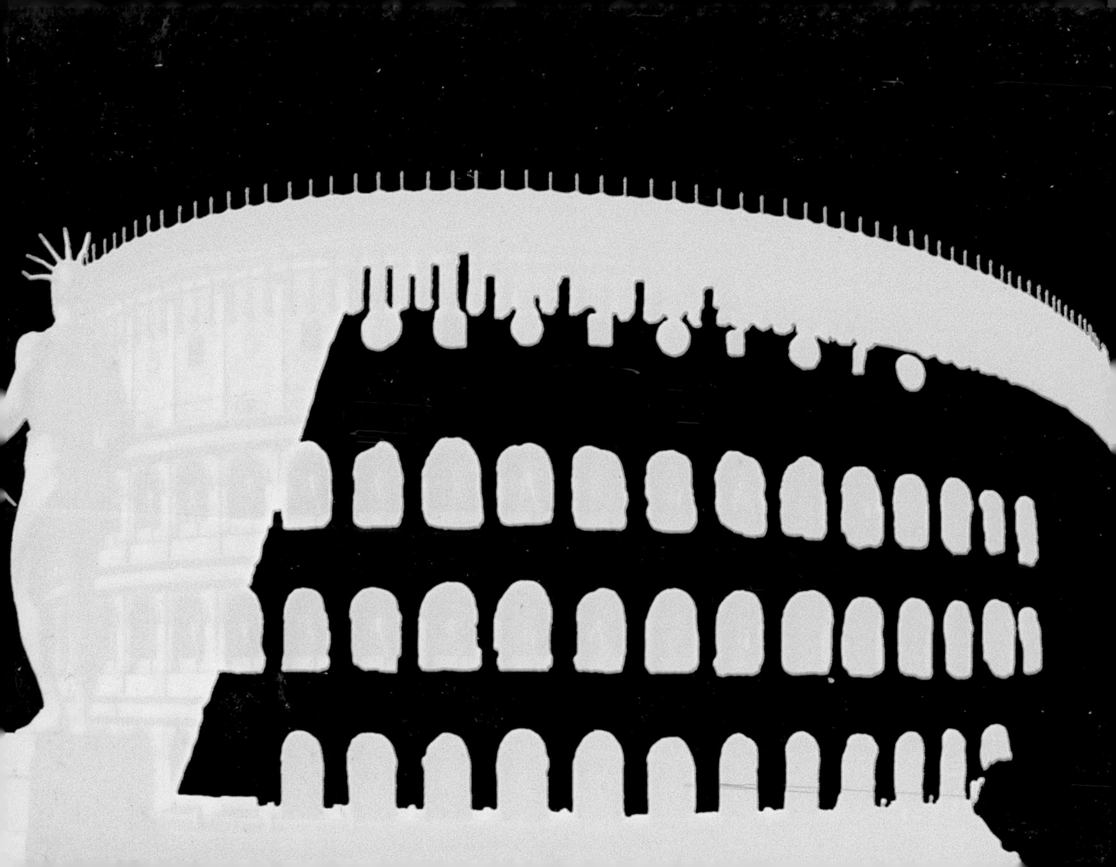

of sailors sent up from the naval base at Misenum, on the Gulf of Naples.

During shows the arena would be surrounded by a metal mesh carried on poles and spiked with elephant tusks; the top of the mesh was furbished with ivory rollers, so that animals could not get a foothold there and escape from the arena.

Just in case, the niches in the podium at the foot of the steps were always full of archers, ever ready to intervene.

The last show of which we have certain knowledge was held in 523 AD under Theodoric, King of the Ostrogoths. It consisted only of animal hunts, for gladiator fighting had been abolished in 438 AD.

A complex system of passages and rooms extended beneath the arena: it was probably constructed under Domitian, after it had been decided that no further 'naval battles' would be staged there. These underground rooms contained facilities and stored the stage equip-

Aerial view of the Colosseum

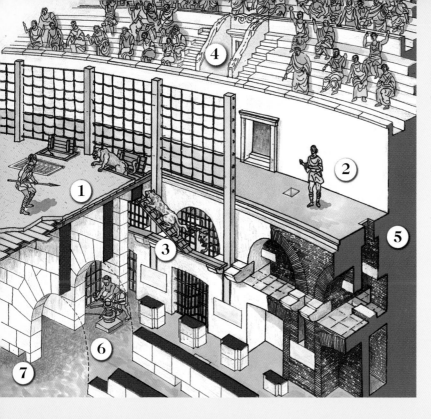

UNDERGROUND ROOMS OF THE COLOSSEUM

1. Arena
2. Balteus
3. Animal route from overhead gangway to ramp
4. Cavea and gradin sectors
5. Skylight
6. Elevators for the beasts
7. Underground level

ment for the shows: the scenery was often very elaborate, especially for the hunts, when the stage managers did not fight shy of creating hills, woods, and even small lakes. For men and animals, genuine 'elevators' were made to function, by using counterweights. The animals, in particular, were first driven along the corridors by their handlers and made to enter cages, which were then raised to a higher level, where the cage would open. The animals could thus step out onto a gangway connected to a ramp, with a trap door at its upper end, from which they would exit into the open, ready for the show.

We are told that on one occasion this system was used to bring a hundred lions into the arena at one and the same moment: their combined roar was so loud that the noisy crowd was frightened into instant silence. The gladiators were able to reach the arena direct from their main 'barracks' (*Ludus Magnus*), situated by the side of the Colosseum, by using an underground passage leading to the amphitheater's underground spaces.

Death of St. Ignatius, Bishop of Antiochia in the 2nd century A.D., first Christian to die as a martyr in the Flavian Amphitheatre

THE GREAT SQUARE OF THE COLOSSEUM

Overshadowed by the immense mass of the amphitheater, **the great Square of the Colosseum** assumed its final monumental appearance with the building of **the Temple of Venus and Rome**, and this layout has been substantially preserved right down to our own day. Ordained and possibly also designed by Hadrian, this temple, dedicated to the divine ancestress of the Julian family and to the city, mistress of the world, was inaugurated in 135 AD and then reconstructed by Maxentius round about 310 AD, after it had been destroyed by fire. It had two apses, standing back to back at the center of a broad terrace on the Velian hill (which at that time stretched beyond today's Via dei Fori Imperiali, from the Palatine hill towards the Esquiline) and was surrounded on at least two sides by porticoes.

The remains of the 'vestibule' of Nero's Golden House were torn down to make room for this temple and even the **Colossus of Nero** had to be shifted. Twelve pairs of elephants were used to move it.

At the beginning of the road which leaves the Square of the Colosseum to run down into the Forum, there was a fountain built in the middle of the 1st century AD, which had a shape rather like one of the *metae* or turning points in the Circus that the chariots had to race round: it therefore came to be known as **Meta Sudans**, the Turn of Sweat.

The last monument added to adorn this great square was **the Arch of Constantine**. As its inscription records, it was erected in 312 AD by the Senate and People of Rome in honour of the Emperor, who had liberated the city and the state from the 'tyrant' Maxentius by his victory in the battle of the Milvian Bridge. The arch was richly decorated with sculpture taken from earlier monuments erected by Trajan, Hadrian and Marcus Aurelius in the 2nd century, and only the small reliefs which run round the whole monument actually depict events in which Constantine himself was involved.

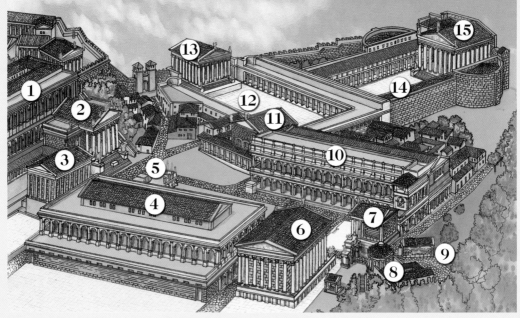

THE FORUM ROMANUM AT THE TIME OF AUGUSTUS

1 – *Tabularium*
2 – Temple of Concord
3 – Temple of Saturn
4 – Basilica Julia
5 – *Rostra*

6 – Temple of Castor
and Pollux
7 – Temple of Divus
Julius
8 – Temple of Vesta

9 – *Regia*
10 – Basilica Aemilia
11 – Curia
12 – The Forum
of Caesar

13 – Temple of Venus
Genetrix
14 – Temple of Augustus
15 – Temple of Mars
Ultor

THE FORUM ROMANUM

The **Forum Romanum** was the commercial, religious, political and legal center of the city, at any rate throughout the Republic, and remained a sacred and monumental area throughout antiquity. Its origins are related the coalescing into a city of the primitive villages which had grown up on the higher parts of the surrounding hills.

The valley of the Forum, lying between the Palatine, the Capitol and the first slopes of the Viminal and the Quirinal, must itself have been affected, albeit marginally, by the presence of some modest nuclei of huts and by an extensive burial ground, dating back to the late bronze age and the early iron age. Around about the end of the 7th century BC, the **Cloaca Maxima** drained away its stagnant waters and it could thus be formally laid out and receive its first 'paving'.

From that time onwards, the part of the valley lying at the foot of the Capitol was set aside for political functions (with the construction of the **Curia**, for the meetings of the Senate, and the **Comitium**, for the assemblies of the people), while the remainder, much larger, came to play the part of the 'square' (the *Forum* in the proper sense of the term), where shops and market stalls intermingled with the city's oldest sanctuaries, of **Vesta**, **Saturn**, **Janus** and **Castor and Pollux**. A small sanctu-

ary consisting of an altar, an honorary column and a tufa block with an inscription dating back to the 6th century BC was interpreted as being the grave of the legendary founder, Romulus, and protected with big slabs of black stone (**lapis niger**).

The **Via Sacra** crossed the whole length of the square, whence it ascended to the Temple of Jupiter Optimus Maximus on the Capitol.

The construction of the first basilicas during the 2nd century BC (the *Porcia*, the oldest, the *Opimia*, the *Sempronia*, and most importantly the *Basilica Aemilia*) further emphasized the Forum's character as a political and administrative center, and it gradually assumed its definitive appearance. The stages in this process were: the building of the **Tabularium**, seat of the state archives on the slopes of the Capitol (80 BC), providing the square with a monumental backdrop;

Detail of the Tabularium, State Archive of Rome

The Forum Square, reconstruction

the moving of the Curia and the *Rostra* (the platform from which the magistrates addressed the people) and the erection of the **Basilica Julia** in front of the Basilica Aemilia by Caesar, marking off the long sides of the square; and finally, the positioning of the Temple of Divine Caesar, ordained by Augustus, in order to close off the fourth side of the square.

The structure of the square remained unchanged for a long time. The construction of new buildings, such as **the Temple of Vespasian and Titus** and that of **Antoninus and Faustina**, built by Antoninus Pius in memory of his wife Faustina, who died in 141 BC, and subsequently dedicated by the Senate to the emperor himself, respected the Augustan layout. The only breach in this convention was the erection of a gigantic equestrian statue of Domitian in the center of the square.

The Forum square: in the foreground columns of the Temple of Castor and Pollux; in the background the Arch of Septimius Severus

Only from the 3rd century AD onwards was the Forum area once again invaded by commemorative and honorary monuments: **the Arch of Septimius Severus**, squeezed in between the *Rostra* and the Curia, the **seven honorary columns** lined up along the south side of the square, in front of the Basilica Julia, and the **monuments** commemorating the **Tenth Anniversary** (*decennalia*) **of the Tetrarchy**.

Indeed, it fell to one of these columns, the one raised in 608 AD in honour of the Byzantine Emperor Phocas, to become the last monument to be added to the Forum. But by that time

Arch of Titus: triumph and the spoil from the Temple at Jerusalem

the millenary glory of what had once been the most important place in Rome had long since faded away.

Plautus, in his comedy *Curculio*, has left us a very vivid and fascinating picture of life in the Forum under the Republic, revealing the characteristics of each place, according to the people frequenting it: 'There in the Comitium, where the judges sit and the orators make their speeches from the platform, you can see the perjurers, the liars and the braggarts;

down there in the square near the statue of Marsyas, are the advocates, the litigants and the witnesses; beside the shops, old and new, in front of the basilica are the strumpets, the bankers, the usurers and the brokers; in the lowest part of the Forum, the serious-minded and the gentlemen who conduct themselves quietly; in the middle, near the canal, the good-for-nothings (*canalicolae*), parasites waiting for a tip from the rich and drunkards; higher up are the gossips and scandal-mongers. Behind the Temple of Castor and the Vicus Tuscus, the criminals and the men of bad fame collect; in the Velabrum are the bakers, butchers, fortune-tellers and dancers; beside the Fountain of Juturna the sick, who drink the miraculous waters; nearby, in the fish market, the bonviveurs. Everywhere the rabble of the idle vagabonds, the men about town - the type that are either deep in gaming or spreading

View of the eastern area of the Forum Romanum, from the Palatine hill

Base of the column of the "Decennalia": relief with sacrificial procession

false rumors and passing pompous judgments on affairs of state...'

But alongside this teeming everyday life in the Forum there was always also another, more or less official life of public affairs and activities. It was here that the magistrates had their official seats and offices; the Consuls and the Senators in the Curia, the Tribunes in the Comitium, the Praetors in the courts; it was from the platform of the *Rostra* that magistrates and candidates for a political career harangued the crowd; and it was in the

Temple of Antoninus and Faustina, detail of the colonnade

Comitium that the people elected their magistrates, and in the Curia that the Senators met.

Religious processions and sacrifices to the gods took place here, as did the grand funerals, sometimes stopping before the *Rostra*, from which laudatory speeches were made in honour of the dead (among them the most famous of all: Mark Antony's speech in honour of Caesar). The gladiatorial shows offered free of charge to the people also took place in the square prior to the building of the amphitheaters. Especially famous among

The Forum Romanum from sou detail with honorary columns

these is the fight organized by Caesar as aedile in 65 BC, when no less than 320 pairs of gladiators took part. Just as famous was the banquet that Caesar gave on the occasion of his triumph in 45 BC, which lasted for several days and catered for 22,000 guests.

The Forum Romanum, at night: in the foreground the Temple of Saturn

THE TEMPLES OF SATURN AND CONCORD

Tradition has it that **the Temple of Saturn** was begun during the last years of the kings and inaugurated at the beginning of the Republic (498/7 AD) and it was venerated as one of the most ancient shrines of Rome. But its appearance today is that given it by a restoration late in the 3rd century AD made necessary by an outbreak of fire. Its huge base encloses a space that was intended for use as the State Treasury, the *Aerarium*.

At the foot of the staircase leading up to the temple entrance, Augustus, in 20 BC, set up a tall column (the *Miliarum Aureum*) on which were inscribed, in letters of gilt bronze, the distances from Rome to the principal cities of the Empire. At the column, which was considered as the center (*umbilicus*) of Rome, there commenced the *Clivus Capitolinus*, which was an extension of the Via Sacra and climbed the Capitol right up to the Temple of Jupiter, passing in front of **the Temple of Vespasian and Titus**, which was begun by Titus in honour of his deified father and completed by his brother and successor, Domitian. Another building along the Clivus was **the Portico of the Consenting Gods** (*Dei Consentes*), which housed gilt bronze statues of the twelve Olympian gods grouped in pairs according to the classical tradition. Next to the Temple of Vespasian there stood **the Temple of Concord**, which was likewise built up against the Tabularium, or state archives. This temple was attributed to Marcus Furius Camillus, who was said to have had it built in 367 BC to commemorate the peace settlement achieved that year by Patricians and Plebeians. Frequently repaired and eventually completely reconstructed by Tiberius, this temple has the distinctive feature of a *cella* arranged in the longitudinal direction. Ancient authors often noted the fact that the many pictures and statues by famous artists kept in this temple had turned it into a museum.

On this side, directly facing the square, was **the platform of the *Rostra***, decorated with the bronze prows taken from the ships of the Volscians at the end of the 4th century BC. Opposite the Temple of Concord stood **the Arch of Septimius Severus**, which was erected by the Senate and People of Rome in 202 AD to commemorate the emperor, who had extended the boundaries of the Empire as far as Mesopotamia.

THE BASILICA AEMILIA

Facing directly onto the Forum, **the Basilica Aemilia**, sole survivor of the Republican basilicas, delimited its northern side, together with the Curia building on the other side of the ancient road known as the Argiletum. Beyond the Curia, the Tullianum, or 'Mamertine' Prison, lay at the foot of the mass of the Arx Capitolina, the view of which was partially obscured by the Arch of Septimius Severus and crowned by the Temple of Juno Moneta.

The purpose of Basilica Aemilia was to provide visitors to the Forum with a comfortable and sheltered place where, during the winter and also in case of bad weather in summer, it would be possible

Basilica Aemilia, relief with a bucranium (ox-skull)

to carry out at least some of the functions that normally took place in the open, especially those connected with the administration of justice and business in general.

The Basilica was actually built in 179 BC by the Censors Marcus Aemilius Lepidus and Marcus Fulvius Nobilior immediately to the rear of a row of public shops (*tabernae*) intended for use by bankers. Subsequently modified on many occasions (lastly by Augustus in 14 BC and by Tiberius in 22 AD), it ended up by incorporating these shops in its ground floor portico, which consisted of a series of sixteen arches spanning between pilasters with half-engaged columns, and supported another similar portico on the upper floor. The interior of the basilica consisted of four aisles with intervening rows of columns, and during the reign of Augustus it received a splendid marble floor. This marble still preserves traces of the fire that destroyed the basilica in 410 AD during the sack of the city by the Visigoths under Alaric.

Basilica Aemilia, entrance's arch

In front of its steps, a small round *sacellum* was dedicated to Cloacina, divinity of the Cloaca Maxima, which runs right underneath. It is said that it marks the point where the Romans and the Sabines made peace and purified themselves after the battle fought in the Forum following the famous 'rape' of the Sabine women.

Basilica Aemilia, frieze showing Rome's origins

THE TEMPLES OF DIVUS JULIUS AND OF CASTOR AND POLLUX

After the murder of Caesar on 15 March 44 BC, the Senate at once decreed solemn honors to the dictator's memory and erected an altar and honorary column on the site where his body had been cremated. It was not until 31 BC, however, that Octavian, Caesar's adoptive son and heir, began to build a temple there, which was completed two years later, in 29, and dedicated to **Divus Julius**, the Deified Caesar. An interesting detail is the recess built into the front of the podium to accommodate the existing altar, which was then walled in to gain the space for an orators' platform above it.

This platform, the New *Rostra*, was adorned with the bronze rams taken from the ships of Antony and Cleopatra after the Battle of Actium.

The temple was flanked by two arches, one on the south side in memory of the Battle of Actium, the other, on the opposite side, ordained by the Senate to celebrate the restitution to the Emperor Augustus of the Legionary Standards, captured from the Triumvir Crassus by the Parthians during the Battle of Carrhae. It is possible that this was later dedicated to his two nephews and heirs, the princes Gaius and Lucius Caesar. Next to Caesar's temple there stood **the Temple of Castor and Pollux**, which had occupied this position ever since the early part of the 5th century BC. Legend attributes its construction to a war fought against Etruscans and Latins, when two youths of extraordinary beauty and stature were seen riding, lance in rest, at the head of the Roman cavalry, leading it to victory. Almost at the same moment two identical youths were seen in the

Marble portrait of the queen Cleopatra

Forum, dismounting from sweating horses and leading them to drink at the Fountain of Juturna; to those who asked them for news of the battle, they told how the Romans had won the day. Then they vanished, and all who had seen them were ready to swear that they were none other than the Dioscuri, Castor and Pollux, the sons of Jupiter.

Aulus Postumius Albinus, who was in command of the cavalry on the day of this portentous vision (15 July 499 BC), therefore vowed a temple to the twin demigods, and it was opened by his son fifteen years later. Over the years it was frequently restored and enlarged, the last time in the 6th century AD, when the young Tiberius gave in its final form, to which belong the three columns that are still standing. Built into its base were several shops housing the activities of jewelers, money changers, and even barbers.

THE TEMPLE OF VESTA AND THE ARCH OF AUGUSTUS

At the point in the Forum, where the ground begins to rise towards the slopes of the Palatine, there stood a temple that was of the utmost importance for the city and her population, for it was dedicated to the goddess who was protectress of the family and thus also of the State: **the Temple of Vesta**, traditionally attributed to Numa Pompilius, one of the first kings of Rome. Within it the Vestal Virgins guarded the sacred and eternal flame, symbol of the eternal life of the city. Stored away in the innermost shrine of this temple and equally jealously guarded, the city also preserved numerous sacred objects, including the Palladium, the wooden image of Pallas Athena, that, as legend would have it, Aeneas had brought from Troy as pledge and warranty of empire. According to some authors,

Golden coin with the portrait of the Emperor Augustus

this temple was round in plan because it had originally been built on the model of a hut, the oldest type of hearth and home known in Italy, and had an opening in the roof to let out the smoke generated by the fire. It was frequently rebuilt following destruction by fire, the last time at the end of the 2nd century AD by Julia Domna, wife of the Emperor Septimius Severus. Opposite the Temple of Vesta, astride the *Vicus Vestae* just before it joins the Via Sacra, rose **the Arch of Augustus**, and right in front of this, a small fountain with a circular basin made of white marble. The triple arch was erected by the Senate to commemorate Octavian's victory over Antony and Cleopatra at Actium, in 31 BC. Its middle passageway was vaulted. It is believed that the lists of consuls and records of all those generals who had obtained the honour of a triumph since the beginning of the Republic (*fasti*) were engraved on special marble panels on the inner walls of the arch. At the back, behind the imposing mass of **the Temple of Castor and Pollux** which stood over the Arch, were the buildings of the Imperial Palaces on the Palatine, which faced onto the Forum.

Aureus with the portrait of Antony

THE HOUSE OF THE VESTAL VIRGINS

The House of the Vestal Virgins, which rose immediately adjacent to the Temple of Vesta, was the home and official residence of the priestesses charged with guarding the sacred fire that burned in the temple and performing the rites connected with the cult of the hearth. The Vestal Virgins were six in number; they entered as novices between the age of six and ten, and remained for thirty years under vows of strict chastity. They were chosen by the

supreme religious authority of the State, the *Pontifex Maximus*; at first only Patricians were eligible, but later they could be chosen also from among the Plebeian families. The Vestal Virgins received a rich dowry from the State, and they were allotted every honour, including that of being accompanied by lictors, a privilege they shared with the consuls. Such was their sacred dignity that if by chance a condemned criminal happened to cross their path, he was automatically reprieved. But they also lived under the menace of a tremendous punishment, for any priestess who allowed the fire to go out or became untrue to her vow of chastity would be buried alive (with a loaf of bread and a lamp) in a small underground chamber in the 'field of the wicked' (*Campus Sceleratus*) just outside the walls on the Quirinal. The House, which has been considered as the prototype of present-day monastic convents, was organized around a large courtyard kept as a garden and surrounded on all

The House of the Vestal Virgins seen from the Palatine hill

sides by a portico. All of the rooms opened onto these galleries, which also gave access to the other spaces of the house, including the quarters of the servants. Self-sufficient in every respect, the house was well appointed and one can still recognize the kitchen, the flour mill, and the ovens. The private rooms were situated on the upper floor, complete with baths and heating facilities, while one of the long sides on the ground floor included a *sacellum* dedicated to the tutelary gods (*Lares*); it was flanked by three rooms on either side, the offices of the six Vestal Virgins. The large room on the opposite side, is thought to have been a *triclinium*.

The building of irregular form located to the south of the House of the Vestals was the Royal Palace (**Regia**), traditionally thought to have been the residence of King Numa, seat of the *Pontifex Maximus* until Augustus donated it to the Vestals.

In front of the House of the Vestals on the other side of the Via Sacra is an imposing monument, consisting of a round central part topped by a dome, with a concave facade containing four niches for the housing of statues and two lateral sections projecting forward on either side. The portal

The so-called Temple of Divus Romulus. The great bronze door is the original one

is flanked by two porphyry columns with capitals in white marble. The large bronze door is original, still perfectly preserved. The building is commonly identified as the **Temple of Divus Romulus**, the son of Maxentius, who died young in 307 BC and was deified. It is, however, very likely that a new identification must be ascribed, though this is still the subject of debate, and it is probably the reworking of a previous temple.

THE BASILICA OF MAXENTIUS

The Emperor Maxentius never saw his basilica finished. He died on the banks of the Tiber at the Milvian Bridge after the famous battle against Constantine in 312 AD. So it was Constantine who inaugurated the last and biggest of the Roman basilicas, after incorporating a few changes of his own. The edifice, one of Imperial Rome's most grandiose, occupied most of the Velia, overlooking the Forum from the east. The basilica covers an area of 100m x 65m, and rests on a large artificial platform built into the side of the hill in the place formerly occupied by the triple portico which had served as the vestibule of Nero's Golden House and

The Basilica of Maxentius, detail of the northern side

was later converted into warehouses and shops for luxury goods and rarities imported from the East. It contained a large central nave terminating in an apse on the west side, flanked by two smaller aisles. These were not roofed by means of beams laid horizontally on the columns, but by cross vaults springing from pilasters in the manner that had by then been in use for over a century in the great 'basilicas' of the bath buildings. This made it possible for the central part of the building to rise to a height of 35 m above the floor; the extraordinary simplicity with which this result was obtained, together with the extreme clarity of spaces, right up to the patterning of the coffering on the ceiling, conferred upon the interior a wonderful sense of harmony.

A colossal statue of Constantine in marble and gilt bronze occupied the west apse.

At the end of the 4th century AD, a grand new entrance was opened onto the Via Sacra on the south side, and the addition of a deep apse with niches in the central arcade of the right aisle altered the orientation of the basilica, now perpendicular to its previous axis.

This magnificent roof fell in 1349 as the result of an earthquake. Just one of the eight columns (20 m high) forming part of the pilasters remained in its original position until 1614, when Pope Paul V removed it (using sixty horses for the purpose) to the square of Santa Maria Maggiore.

Portrait statue of the Emperor Maxentius

THE IMPERIAL FORA

The splendid group of monuments that constitute **the Imperial Fora** originally came into being to meet the need for more space than was available in the old political and administrative center, as the population of the city multiplied and the amount of business to be transacted increased. The process began towards the end of the Republican period in the 1st century BC.

Caesar was the first to think of enlarging the time-honored square of the Forum Romanum by building a new Forum immediately adjacent to it and at the very foot of the citadel (*Arx*) on the Capitol; this forum later became known by the dictator's name (***Forum Julium***). It had the absolutely regular form of an elongated rectangle, all planned on the model of the public squares (*agorai*) of Hellenistic cities, with porticoes and shops on three sides and a temple in the center.

Following the example of his adoptive father, Augustus, some fifty years later, built another Forum of practically the same size somewhat to the east, between the Forum of Caesar and the Quirinal. His forum was separated from the ill-famed district of the Suburra by a high stone wall that also served to protect it from the violent fires that frequently ravaged the Suburra. The only novelty introduced by **the Forum of Augustus** was constituted

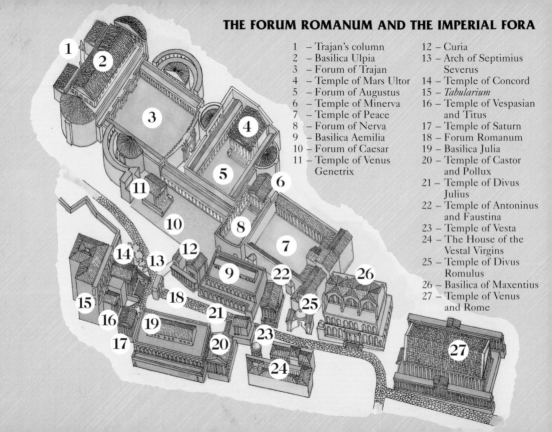

THE FORUM ROMANUM AND THE IMPERIAL FORA

1 – Trajan's column
2 – Basilica Ulpia
3 – Forum of Trajan
4 – Temple of Mars Ultor
5 – Forum of Augustus
6 – Temple of Minerva
7 – Temple of Peace
8 – Forum of Nerva
9 – Basilica Aemilia
10 – Forum of Caesar
11 – Temple of Venus Genetrix
12 – Curia
13 – Arch of Septimius Severus
14 – Temple of Concord
15 – *Tabularium*
16 – Temple of Vespasian and Titus
17 – Temple of Saturn
18 – Forum Romanum
19 – Basilica Julia
20 – Temple of Castor and Pollux
21 – Temple of Divus Julius
22 – Temple of Antoninus and Faustina
23 – Temple of Vesta
24 – The House of the Vestal Virgins
25 – Temple of Divus Romulus
26 – Basilica of Maxentius
27 – Temple of Venus and Rome

by the fact that its sides were bounded by two large covered hemicycles fronted by porticoes with a double order of columns and decorated internally by engaged columns and niches containing statues.

With the two new Fora of Caesar and Augustus Rome's center had become adequate in size to meet her needs, all the more so when, immediately after his triumph in the Jewish War, the Emperor Vespasian constructed a **Temple of Peace** in the vicinity of the Forum of Augustus, using it to display the booty taken from the Temple at Jerusalem. By the time he had surrounded it with gardens and a three-sided portico, he had in effect built a new forum, though it was not officially called so until much later. When Domitian, subsequently, used the space left free between the Forum of Augustus and the Temple of Peace to construct yet another forum (known as the **Forum of Nerva**, who inaugurated it in 97 AD, or, more popularly,

Forum of Trajan: the Basilica Ulpia and Trajan's Column

Forum of Trajan, reconstruction of the Basilica Ulpia and detail of Trajan's column

as the '*Transitorium*', on account of its leading from one into the other), he had not only solved all problems of layout and direct communications, but had also brought to life a unique and continuous complex, well worthy of being the center of the sovereign city of the world.

This did not deter Trajan (98-117AD) from adding the forum that now bears his name, entrusting its construction to Apollodorus, a famous Damascan architect.

*Bust of the Emperor Trajan
(Ankara, Archaeological
Museum)*

Frieze with Victories from the main nave of the Basilica Ulpia

In order to create it, the high ground that joined the Capitol to the Quirinal and entire streets of houses were swept away, including some buildings and monuments of a certain value. But this forum served to put the administrative center and the old city into direct communication with

Detail of Trajan's column

Forum Transitorium, south-eastern wall: "le Colonnacce"

the 'new' city that had grown up in the Campus Martius area, thus realizing a dream already cherished by Augustus.

The Forum of Trajan was the last of the Imperial Fora, but it was also the most grandiose

Trajan's Market: general view

and resplendent of them all. 300m long and 185m wide, it also included the Basilica Ulpia, so called after one of the emperor's other names, libraries and a magnificent honorary column. An inscription placed at the base of the column is still legible, informing us that the column's height, of about 40 meters, corresponds to the height of the hill which was leveled at that point.

THE FORUM OF CAESAR

Basalt bust of Gaius Julius Caesar (Berlin, Staatmuseum)

When Caesar decided to construct a new forum beside the old, there were serious problems that had to be solved before his plan could be executed. Apart from purchasing and demolishing the numerous houses that occupied the chosen area, a great deal of earth had to be removed to level the site, a long stairway had to be cut in the slope of the Capitol, and the neighboring Senate House had to be moved, together with all its accessory buildings. The enormous cost of all this (the sole purchase of the land called for a hundred million *sestertii*) was met out of the vast spoils of the Gallic Wars. Particular care was paid to the design and construction of the most important monument in this Forum, **the temple** dedicated to **Venus Genetrix**, which Caesar himself had vowed to erect on the eve of the Battle of Pharsalus against his rival Pompey. Venus was considered to be the divine progenitrix of the family to which Caesar belonged, for she was said to be the mother of Aeneas, the Trojan hero, who - after his flight from the

burning city and many years of wandering over the Mediterranean - settled at last in Latium at the mouth of the Tiber. There, before he could marry Lavinia the daughter of the king of Latium, he had to fight a final battle against the king of Ardea, Turnus. But Aeneas won and he and Lavinia had a son, Iulus, who was said to be the ancestor of the Julians. The temple was inaugurated on 26 September in the year 46 BC, and Caesar adorned it with numerous works of art, including two pictures by Thymomachus of Byzantium, which he had bought for 80 talents, six collections of engraved gems and a jeweled cuirass he had taken in Britain. The temple also contained a statue of Caesar and another of Cleopatra.

As regards the cult statue itself, it was the work of the Greek sculptor Archesilaos and showed Venus with a cupid on her shoulders and holding a child in her arms. It stood in the apse which opened in the rear wall of the temple's *cella*.

THE FORUM OF AUGUSTUS

Augustus took his decision to build a new forum by means of a vow he made to Mars before the Battle of Philippi (42 BC), in which he defeated Brutus and Cassius, the murderers of Caesar. Nevertheless, **the Temple of Mars Ultor** (i.e. Mars the Avenger), the very centerpiece of the Forum, was not inaugurated until forty years later.

Built entirely of Carrara marble, this temple had eight columns on the facade and a like number on both sides, while its pediment was decorated by a high relief which had as its central figure Mars leaning on his lance and standing between Venus (with Eros) and Fortuna; further to the right there was the Goddess Roma and a figure representing the River Tiber, while to the left of Venus one could see Romulus in the act of taking the omen from a flight of birds, followed by a personalization of the Palatine.

Caesar's sword was kept in the cell of this temple, together with the legionary standards which had been lost to the Parthians in the defeat of Crassus, Augustus having succeeded in getting them back.

This forum was dedicated to exalting the emperor and his role as preserver of tradition and embodiment of the city's historical destiny, within a 'providential' design that the gods both desired and protected. A large number of statues of heroes (Aeneas and his son Iulus, Romulus, the kings of Albalonga) and great historical figures (*summi viri*) from Rome's past therefore lined the hemicycles and porticoes.

In the center of the square, in front of the temple, rose the statue of Augustus, represented on a triumphal chariot. Another statue of the emperor, rising to as much as 14m, stood in a sumptuously decorated hall at the end of the portico to the left of the temple. Like the portico itself, this hall terminated against the high wall that separated the forum from the Suburra.

Portrait statue of the Emperor Augustus found at Prima Porta to the north of Rome (Vatican Museum)

THE PALATINE

For the Romans, **the Palatine** had always represented the city's sacred birthplace. All ancient authors agree with the archeological evidence that the hill, isolated from the others and in a position which dominated both the Tiber, right by the Tiber Island, and also the Forum Boarium market, was the site of the legendary 'founding' of Rome and the 'square furrow' ploughed by Romulus on 21 April of the year 754/3 BC. Legend apart, the hill has disclosed the remains of early bronze-age huts, providing incontrovertible evidence of the presence of an inhabited area in the very place to which ancient tradition ascribed the *casa Romuli*, ie the hut of the legendary founder.

This was certainly one and probably also the most important of the villages from which the city of Rome was to evolve over the course of time.

The history of the Palatine is rather obscure during the early centuries of the city's existence and, apart from **Temples of Victory**, **of Jupiter Stator**, **of Jupiter Victor** and of **the Magna Mater**, no public buildings were erected there. On the other hand, many private homes and 'urban' villas were built there by the rich and famous, especially during the last two centuries of the Republic.

In 44 BC Augustus too decided to transfer his home there, where he also ordered the building of a temple dedicated to Apollo, inaugurated in 28 BC.

From then on almost all the emperors went to live on the Palatine, which was gradually transformed into a single, sumptuous royal residence, the archetypal 'palace', a term which derives from the name of the hill, the *Palatium*.

Palatine, Domus Augustana: internal court with fountain and motif of four "peltae" (the shields of the Amazones)

The first true imperial palace was the work of Tiberius, successor of Augustus. He was followed by Caligula, who extended the building as far as the edge of the cliff overlooking the forum, while Claudius and Nero (between 41 and 60 AD) built the so-called **Domus Transitoria**, which soon burnt down in the great Neronian fire of 64 and was never rebuilt. It was Domitian who built a new palace on the ruins and, by occupying also the areas left free by his predecessors, created a new, more grandiose palace.

View of the northern slopes of the Palatine hill: buildings and shops of Neronian age and the archs of the Domus Tiberiana

Domitian's complex, known as the **Domus Augustana**, or House of Augustus (i.e. of the Emperor), consisted basically of a public palace and a private residence, a large stadium or hippodrome, and baths. Extending along the slopes of the hill and up to the summit, with halls and stairways, rooms and peristyles, porticoes, terraces and fountains, the great *domus* was, to put it in the words of the poet Martial, 'one of the most beautiful things in the world, a tall and massive pile composed of seven hills placed one on top of the other, until they touch the sky'.

Septimius Severus, who reigned at the turn of the second and third centuries, artificially extended the level of the hill southwards as far as the stands of the Circus Maximus below, carried on a series of brickwork arcades in two orders, rising to a height of 20 - 30 m.

Right at the bottom of the hill, Severus also erected the famous **Septizodium**, a remarkable multistorey structure, richly adorned with columns, niches and statues and probably animated by the play of running water like a nymphaeum, to greet the eye and invite the admiration of the traveler as he entered Rome by the Via Appia.

Painting from the "House of Livia" on the Palatine

After Septimius Severus there were no more important works on the Palatine except a temple built by Elagabalus, in the 3rd century AD, in a corner opposite the Colosseum. Rather, starting with Diocletian at the beginning of the 4th century, the

Palatine, palace of Domitian: the so-called stadium

emperors actually began to desert it. This abandonment became definitive when Constantine transferred the capital of the empire to Byzantium.

Domus Flavia, western nymphaeum: elliptical fountain with niches

Stadium of the Palatine, detail of the northern portico

THE DOMUS AUREA

In 64 AD most of the center of Rome was destroyed in an enormous fire which started in the area of the Circus Maximus and reached the top of the Esquiline. While the story blaming Nero for the fire gained currency as a result of the emperor's already bad reputation, the destruction wrought by the disaster certainly made it easier to construct the most extensive **domus** ever built, awarded the epithet **aurea** for the magnificence of its decoration and the opulence of its buildings. The architects engaged for the building of the palace, *Severus* and *Celer*, decided to adopt the format of a country villa right in the center of Rome, and the 2nd century historian Tacitus notes that the *domus* was admired by people at the time not so much for its precious materials, already seen in the previous palace, as for its woods, pastures and lakes, the largest of which filled the site now occupied by the Colosseum. The buildings therefore covered a vast area extending from the Palatine to the Oppian, at the foot of the Celian.

Suetonius, author of the biographies of the first twelve Caesars, recounts that the *atrium* of the palace consisted of a triple portico which was a thousand paces long (about 1,500 meters) and contained

Domus Aurea, painting with the representation of Achilles among King Lycomedes'daughters, in the palace of Scyros (room nr. 119)

the Colossus, a statue of Nero 120 feet high (35 meters). The decoration of the interiors made use of all kinds of precious materials: gold and ivory were everywhere, and the flowers in the paintings were set with precious stones. The ceilings of the banqueting halls were fitted with sliding panels of ivory, so that flowers and perfumes could be scattered onto the diners from above. The pictorial decoration, entrusted to the painter *Fabullus*, was in an opulent, magnificent style, depicting figures framed in geometric patterns which were endlessly enriched

19	Cryptoporticus of the western wing	92	Cryptoporticus of the eastern wing
20	Peristilium	116-117-118	Rooms of the eastern wing
36-35-47-49	Rooms of the western wing	122-123-125-126	Rectangular and cruciform rooms
50	Corridor called "of the eagles"		opening onto the octagonal hall
44-45	Nymphaeum of Ulysses and Polyphemus	119	Room of Achilles at Scyros
70	Room with painted false windows	124	Nymphaeum
79	Corridor	128	Octagonal hall
80	Room with golden vault	129	Room of Hector and Andromache

by the motifs of plants and imaginary creatures. It is the Oppian Hill sector of this imposing residence that we know best. Built on platforms overlooking the valley in which the Colosseum was later to rise, it was divided into three main blocks.

The two lateral ones were based on the traditional nucleus of the peristyle villa, their rooms distributed around a porticoed garden. The central block, separated from the others by large pentagonal gardens, was, on the other hand, built around an octagonal hall, the vault of which was supported by octagonal

Coin with the portrait of Nero

pillars, with a circular light-well in the center. The sides of the octagon gave onto rectangular rooms, which all looked back towards the center of the hall, where a statue was probably placed, lit to striking effect from the light well above. This was certainly one of the banqueting halls of the *domus*, perhaps the main one which - Suetonius recounts - rotated continuously on its own axis, like the earth.

After Nero's death in 68 AD, the emperors who succeeded him returned large parts of

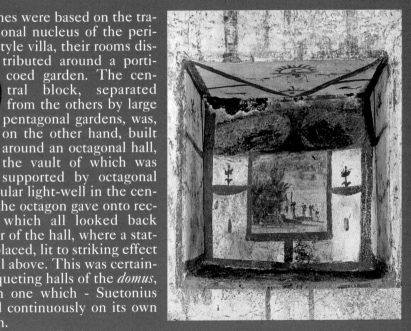

Domus Aurea, niche with a painted false window

the Domus Aurea to the city. Thus, on top of Nero's palace, rose public monuments like the Colosseum and all the buildings connected with it (eg the gladiators' barracks, their hospital and the depot for the stage equipment used during the spectacles), the public baths built by Titus and also the state mint (*Moneta*).

The last sector to be dismantled was the luxurious Oppian Hill area which, having been stripped of all its recyclable materials, was interred for the construction of the Baths of Trajan.

Domus Aurea, flying figures in the vault of the room of Hector and Andromache (n. 129)

THE CIRCUS MAXIMUS

Tradition had it that the first *circus* on this site was built by King Tarquinius Priscus to mark the place where the rape of the Sabine women had been perpetrated. However this may be, **the Circus Maximus** was used for chariot racing and can be considered as the largest building ever put up for entertainment purposes. Indeed, when the *circus* attained its greatest size, in the heyday of the imperial age, it measured no less than 600m in length and 200m in width, and could accommodate up to 300,000 spectators. The last of the major reconstructions of the *circus* was undertaken by Trajan at the beginning of the 2nd century AD, though it was later enlarged by Caracalla and restored by Constantine, while Constans, as late as 357 AD, had it adorned with an Egyptian obelisk (attributed to Thutmosis III), which thus came to make a pair with the one (bearing the cartouche of Ramses II) that Augustus had erected at the center of the *spina*, the characteristic barrier that ran down the middle of the arena, thus defining the circuit that the chariots had to complete seven times before reaching the finishing line. The seating area was divided into three sections by horizontal gangways, interrupted on Palatine side by the great imperial 'box', which was in direct communication with the palaces on the top of the hill. But a part of the seating, presumably the topmost rows, must have been sustained by wooden structures,

Mosaic with horses and grooms; the horses represent the four rival factions of the circus (Sousse - Tunisia)

because the records apprise us of frequent collapses: one such disaster killed 1,112 spectators in the time of Antoninus Pius and another, under Diocletian, no less than 13,000. The Circus Maximus had a long life. Races were still being organized there in the 5th century AD, the last spectacle to be put on being the one sponsored by Totila, King of the Ostrogoths, in 549. The two obelisks were unearthed in 1588 and Pope Sixtus V had them removed and re-erected, one in Piazza del Popolo and the other in front of the side entrance of St. John in Lateran, where they can still be seen today.

The circus and the spectators (Tunis, Museum of Bardo)

The consul among the factions of the circus. Rome, Basilica of Junius Bassus

THE THEATRE OF MARCELLUS

During the Republic, the censors forbade the construction of permanent theaters, this in deference to the puritan spirit of traditional Roman custom, which saw in theatrical spectacles a danger to public morality: the only theaters permitted were of wood. It was not until the last years of the Republic that Pompey dared to put up the first theater built of stone. Pompey's theater was followed by **the Theater of Balbus** and **the Theater of Marcellus**, which occupies a site between the Capitol and the Tiber and is the only one that can still be seen today. It was begun by Caesar and completed by Augustus in 11 BC, when he dedicated it to the memory of his nephew and heir Marcellus.

The theater had a diameter of 130 meters, rose to a height of 30m, and could seat about 15,000 spectators. In the Middle Ages it was used as a fortress by the noble Roman families, and in the 16th century it was transformed into a palace for the Caetani by the architect Baldassarre Peruzzi.

The choice of this site for the theater had been determined by that of the adjoining **Temple of Apollo**, where, already in Republican times, the special games celebrated in honour of the god included the-

atrical spectacles. The original temple was founded in 431 BC, when the cult of Apollo *medicus* (Apollo the healer) was introduced to Rome for the first time as the result of a vow made during a grave outbreak of pestilence. What can be seen today, however, goes back to a radical reconstruction undertaken by the Consul Gaius Sosius in 36 BC. Finely decorated with reliefs and sculptures, the Sosian Temple, as Romans dubbed it, incorporated in the triangular space of its pediment an original Greek sculpture that went back to the 5th century BC and depicted a battle between Amazons. The slightly smaller temple by the side of the Temple of Apollo cannot be attributed with certainty, though there are reasons for thinking that it might be the one that Appius Claudius Caecus, builder of the Via Appia, dedicated to Bellona in 296 BC.

Columns of the Sosian Temple of Apollo

Portrait of Agrippa, Augustus's friend and son-in-law, who erected the first Pantheon

The interior of the Pantheon

THE PANTHEON

A splendid temple in honour of all the Olympian gods was erected in the Campus Martius by Marcus Vipsanius Agrippa, son-in-law and counselor of the Emperor Augustus, between 27 and 25 AD. The temple therefore became known as **the Pantheon**, a Greek name meaning 'of all the Gods'. What we see today, however, preserved substantially just as it was in antiquity, is not Agrippa's original temple, but rather the result of a complete reconstruction undertaken by Hadrian between 118 and 125 AD, the first temple having been destroyed by fire in 80 AD. Wholly different from its predecessor, the new Pantheon had a great circular hall roofed by a hemispherical vault with an opening at the center, 9 m in diameter. The diameter of the hall (and therefore also of the dome) stretches 43.3m and is exactly equal to the greatest height of the building, so that its interior could accommodate a perfect sphere of that diameter. The entrance to the rotunda from the outside is through a traditional *pronaos* with sixteen monolithic columns of Egyptian granite arranged in two orders of eight columns each. The inscription in bronze letters on the architrave (the bronze is modern but set in the original cuttings) records the temple's foundation by

Agrippa in his third consulate. The pediment above the architrave was decorated with reliefs in gilt bronze, and the internal trabeation of the *pronaos* was originally lined with the same material. The bronze was removed by Pope Urban VIII and then used

by Bernini to cast the great baldacchino over the Confessione in St. Peter's. Inside the Pantheon there are numerous other monolithic columns, great rarities, in Numidian yellow and Phrygian purple. The interior survives in its original form, perfectly preserved, and in this respect it is unique among the monuments of antiquity. Pope Boniface IV received the building as a gift from the Byzantine Emperor Phocas in 608 AD and transformed it from a pagan temple into a Christian church, dedicating it to the Madonna and all the martyrs (Santa Maria *ad Martyres*).

The great dome of the Pantheon

THE MAUSOLEUM OF HADRIAN

Following the example of Augustus, who had built a Mausoleum in the Campus Martius, the Emperor Hadrian (117-138 AD) decided to build a monumental tomb for himself and his successors during his lifetime. The resulting **Mausoleum of Hadrian** was erected on the right bank of the Tiber, not far from that of Augustus, in the area occupied by the gardens of the family of the Domitii, near the edge of the Vatican Fields.

Begun around 130 AD, it had a massive cylindrical core, 64m in diameter, the lower part of which was surrounded by a square base completely veneered in marble. An earthen tumulus probably rose above this cylinder, the monument being crowned by a huge central pillar surmounted by a gilt bronze statue of the emperor in a chariot. The building was incomplete when Hadrian died and he could not be buried there until a year later, in 139 AD, after Antoninus Pius had finished the great tomb. To facilitate direct access to the tomb from the Campus Martius, Hadrian also built the bridge to which he gave his family name, the **Pons Aelius**, a greater and more elaborate structure than any of its predecessors. It survived intact until the end of the last century,

Castel Sant'Angelo, night view

though by that time known as **Ponte Sant'Angelo**, but then had to be interfered with to permit construction of the modern Tiber embankments; the two end spans were in fact rebuilt at that time, so that only the three central arches now survive as they were originally built between 130 and 134 AD. The Mausoleum was included by Honorius, at the beginning of the 5th century, in the defensive system of the Aurelian Walls, as a kind of outlying bastion, and perhaps from the 10th century onwards, it was transformed into a fortress, **Castel Sant'Angelo**, serving to defend the Vatican, to which it was linked by a special 'viaduct' (raised passageway).

Aerial view of Castel Sant'Angelo

The Mausoleum of Hadrian, reconstructi

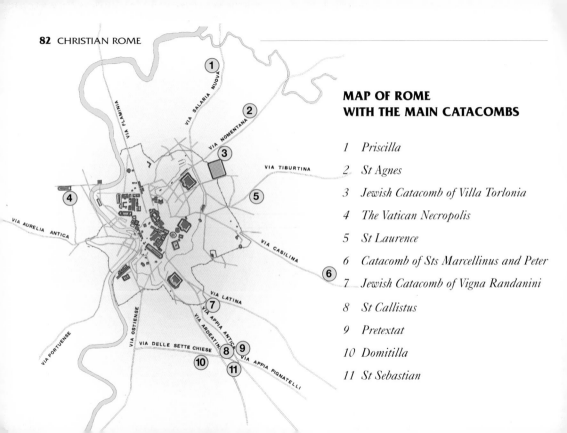

MAP OF ROME
WITH THE MAIN CATACOMBS

1 *Priscilla*

2 *St Agnes*

3 *Jewish Catacomb of Villa Torlonia*

4 *The Vatican Necropolis*

5 *St Laurence*

6 *Catacomb of Sts Marcellinus and Peter*

7 *Jewish Catacomb of Vigna Randanini*

8 *St Callistus*

9 *Pretextat*

10 *Domitilla*

11 *St Sebastian*

CHRISTIAN ROME

Why catacombs?

Outside the walls, among the ancient Roman buildings and residential areas, there developed a subterranean city of the dead, consisting of dozens of kilometers of tunnels, the reign of total darkness. Over the centuries these labyrinths excited the popular imagination. Thus learned traditions also grew up regarding the use of the catacombs as refuges for the early, persecuted Christians. We now know that this cannot have been so, as at the time of the persecutions the catacombs were still at an embryonic stage, located in the midst of pagan tombs and, as such, of common knowledge.

There were many circumstances which brought about the birth of the great Roman catacombs: the constant increase in the population of Rome (estimated by scholars brave enough to attempt such calculations at between 500,000 and 2,000,000 inhabitants at the height of the Empire), the ever-increasing need for burial space (especially with the systematic adoption of the practice of burial, the rite favored by the Christians, as opposed to cremation), the construction of large villas surrounded by cultivated land at the gates of the city, in the places where the public burial grounds had previously been situated, and finally, the fact that tombs were already being located further outside the city in the 2nd century AD.

Therefore Christians, Jews and Pagans all began, from the 3rd century onwards, to dig underneath the tombs and the funerary areas near the city, that thay had purchased or inherited, and which frequently were impossible to use on the surface because all the available space had been occupied by their ancestors.

THE FIRST CHRISTIAN CEMETERIES IN ROME

The earliest Christian catacombs - of which St Callistus is the most famous example - give us a picture of 3rd century Christian society, for which there is no other archeological evidence in Rome. These are subterranean networks of short, fairly regular tunnels (a few hundred meters in length), with the capacity for a few hundred tombs at the most. What may be observed is that they are remarkably uniform and the tombs are very austere. In a few isolated cases the tombs, usually funerary chambers (*cubicula*), are decorated with very simple paintings. This is true even of the tombs of the first popes of Rome, buried in St Callistus.

ST CALLISTUS

The name of the site currently refers to a whole series of various underground cemeteries which were actually independent in ancient times, even though many of their tunnels joined up at a certain point. It would therefore be more correct to refer to the 'St Callistus complex'. Its sprawling network of tunnels extending for many kilometers is situated along the Via Appia Antica, and this cemetery is the closest to Rome of all those in the area. The cemetery of St Callistus is without doubt the most ancient Christian catacomb in

St Callistus, reconstruction of two superimposed gallery levels

Rome. We know that it was the property of the Church right from the start. Pope Zephyrinus (199-217) entrusted its administration to Callistus, the first of his deacons, who succeeded him and died in *222* AD under the persecution of the emperor Alexander Severus.

St Callistus may be regarded as the most important cemetery of the early Christians in Rome, primarily for the number and prestige of the martyrs and canonized bishops who

were buried here. It was thought that anyone buried close to these holy tombs would be greatly helped in attaining the next world, so an impressive network developed of several kilometers of tunnels and cubicula. These burials *apud* or *retro sanctos* (around or behind the saints) were the initial core of the St Callistus complex, which grew into its present form mainly in the course of the 4th century.

The most important points of the whole itinerary and the richest in history, not only of Christian Rome but also of the Universal Church as a whole, are without doubt the **Papal Crypt** and the **Crypt of St Cecilia**.

St Callistus, cubicula of the Sacraments: Jonas being thrown into the sea

Crypt of St Cecilia, reconstruction

A long staircase leads down to a large *cubiculum*, which is at first sight nothing spectacular, but it is actually the first collective burial site of the bishops of Rome.

The chamber is in the form of a large rectangular hall, with twelve loculi and four niches which must have contained urns carved into the longer walls. The shorter side facing the entrance contains only one tomb, a loculus later transformed into a more monumental tomb with marble decorations. The present appearance of the crypt is the result both of alterations linked to the cult of the popes buried here, and of modern restoration work in the attempt to recreate its original appearance, at least in part.

In front of the entrance are the remains of the altar base, with the inscription which Pope Damasus dedicated to this sanctuary. This is one of the most beautiful which he had inscribed, a hymn to the martyrs buried here. The most remarkable of all these is certainly the martyr Cecilia (or *Caecilia* in Latin), about whom we have little substantial information

A narrow passageway to the left of the altar leads into the Crypt of St Cecilia, which contains the remains of paintings from various periods (5th –7th century), which are unfortunately badly damaged.

St Callistus, Crypt of St Cecilia; painting with Saints **The Cubicula of the Sacraments.**

St Callistus, cubicula of the Sacraments: Moses and the miracle of the spring

These are six small funerary chambers situated along one side of a single tunnel, in which can be admired some of the oldest paintings of Christian Rome. These pictures of the greatest simplicity trasmitted a message even to the less well educated among the faithful, expressed by means of biblical scenes from the Old and New Testaments.

THE CATACOMBS OF DOMITILLA

The Catacombs of Domitilla on the Via Ardeatina are the most extensive underground catacombs in Rome, together with those of St Callistus.

Flavia Domitilla, after whom the catacombs are named, was an important landowner in the area. She was the niece of the emperor Domitian, who had her husband put to death and sent her into exile in 95 AD, accusing them of 'atheism and Judaic practices', which has led many historians to believe that the couple might have been Christians.

The only two martyrs who may be attributed with any certainty to the catacomb are the two soldiers Nereus and Achilleus, probably executed during the Diocletian's persecution of Christians in the military (295-298).

Nowadays the tour begins in the great underground basilica built

Reconstruction of the Basilica of Saints Nereus and Achilleus, killed during Diocletian's persecution of Christians in the military

by Pope Damasus (366-384) in honor of the martyrs Nereus and Achilleus.

SAINT SEBASTIAN

At this point on the Via Appia the land sloped steeply in ancient times, creating a natural depression, and there were many stone quarries in the area. The epithet *ad catacumbas*, which was applied in medieval times to the catacombs of St Sebastian, derives from the Greek expression '*katà kumbas*', which means 'by the caves'.
Many graffiti in Latin and in Greek have been found from the mid-3th and the early 4th century, and invoke the Apostles Peter and Paul.
These graffiti, together with other ancient sources, testify that the two Princes of the Apostles were venerated in this place in the mid-3th century, perhaps in the tangible form of certain relics originating from their tombs in the Vatican and on the Via Ostiense. It is

St Sebastian, pagan mausoleums of the 2nd century AD

not clear why the cult of the two Apostles was transferred to this place. According to some scholars, the persecution of Valerian in 257 AD had rendered their tombs inaccessible. The cult on the Appian Way may have grown up around these relics, the nature of which is unknown, becoming a permanent institution. The relics revered in this place could have been brought back to their original location when the basilicas were built over the tombs of the two Apostles.

In the second half of the 4th century a rectangular crypt with an altar at the center, was built over the tomb of the martyr Sebastian. Perhaps an army officer, he was condemned, upon refusal to renounce the Christian faith, to die by being shot through with arrows.

St Sebastian, graffiti with prayers to Peter and Paul

THE BASILICA OF SAINT PETER

The area was known in ancient times as the *Ager Vaticanus*; it was regarded as unhealthy, due to its marshy nature, and it was therefore fairly deserted. Reclaimed in the 1st century AD and added to the imperial possessions, Caligula (37-41) had a circus built on it, later completed by Nero (54-68). According to tradition, it was

St Peter's, façade of Constantine's basilica